Published by Barbour Publishing, Inc., P.O. Box 719, Uhrichsville, Ohio 44683 http://www.barbourbooks.com

 Member of the
Evangelical Christian
Publishers Association

Printed in China.

SO YOU'RE OFF TO COLLEGE

An Essential Guide to Life on Campus

CYNDI BUSER

BARBOUR
PUBLISHING, INC.

WHAT NOT TO BRING TO COLLEGE. . .
TOP TWENTY LIST

1. Your shyness
2. A tuba
3. Very large photos of yourself
4. Your high school sweetheart
5. A full-size refrigerator
6. Your old Lego sets
7. Bad breath
8. All of your dad's socks
9. A bad attitude
10. A big-screen television
11. Your dog
12. Your mom
13. A slide rule (a joke for those over forty)
14. Frozen foods
15. A 1977 *Britannica* set
16. Your high school graduation tassel
17. A large sombrero
18. Any family member's clothing
19. Your "blanky" or "wooby"
20. Drugs

INTRODUCTION

We've been there, done that. We've been to college, even graduate school, and now my husband and I are sending two of our own. As you embark on your new life, you will be filled with many mixed emotions and fears. We are here to tell you that those feelings are very typical and even expected. Although it is important to learn many of life's lessons on your own, let's face it, life is tough enough to figure out. That's why we offer you this book—to make the transition from living with your parents to living on your own a little easier. Use this book as an inspirational, motivational, and informational guide. There are shortcuts, prayers, health tips, study hints, some humor, some Scripture, and even a packing checklist. Have fun with it. We hope it is helpful as you enjoy your college experience.

Cyndi Buser

LEAVING HOME

Dear Jesus,

During this time of transition, help me to find a home in You, wherever I may be, full of Your love, acceptance, and comfort—a place where I know I belong. I'm sure You have amazing things in store for me. Be with my family, too, as they experience big changes as well. Give us Your peace that surpasses all understanding.

Amen.

. . . .

I am the vine; you are the branches.
If a man remains in me and I in him,
he will bear much fruit;
apart from me you can do nothing.
John 15:5

1. FUNNY FEELING IN YOUR STOMACH?

Leaving home for the first time is confusing, emotional, and frightening. Prepare yourself. Going away to college is a gigantic step—a milestone you might say. Look at this step as a challenge and one that will foster tremendous and exciting changes in your development as a person. That funny feeling in your stomach is a natural one.

2. "EEK. . .I'VE GOT A MILLION THINGS TO DO!"

It's kind of overwhelming that you will be moving to another "new home." Give yourself ample time to finish any business before leaving home—say good-byes, write thank-you notes, shop for necessities, pack, and arrange for transportation to school. Start early!

3. "ADIOS, AU REVOIR, SAYONARA—I'M OUTTA HERE!"

Leaving home can be pretty stressful and can put a strain on family relationships. Your parents are also going through an emotional time as you prepare to leave. Do your best to make your last memories with friends and family warm ones. Try to be patient and forgiving.

4. GOT NOTHIN' TO WEAR!

What will I wear? Take clothing appropriate to the climate, campus atmosphere, and your personality. Most colleges are quite casual and sometimes "preppy."

5. BIG WHEEL ON CAMPUS!

On large campuses, bicycles can be lifesavers for transporting you to and from your classes. Get your bicycle in good working order before you leave or buy an old bike with a great lock (a "U" lock). On some campuses rollerblades work well, but check to make sure they are allowed.

6. WARM FUZZIES

Your dorm room will be your new home for a while. Try to pack some personal things that will bring warmth and personality to your new abode. Use posters, pillows, curtains, framed photos, plants, or whatever! Make it personal and homey.

7. PACKING CHECKLIST

Plan your packing carefully—when you're happily settled into your well-appointed dorm room, you'll be thankful you took the extra time. For a checklist of important items, see pages 38–40.

GETTING SETTLED

Dear Father,

You have made all things for me, and I praise You. Guide me through this new experience as I embark on college life. Keep my words, thoughts, and actions worthy of Your love. Hold me close, Lord, and help me to live according to your commandments. You are my Creator, my Redeemer, and my Comforter; I pray to You through Jesus Christ.

Amen.

. . . .

"Love the Lord your God with all your heart
and with all your soul and with all your strength
and with all your mind"; and,
"love your neighbor as yourself."
Luke 10:27

8. "MISS YA, MOM!"

Being homesick is nothing new. Most of your classmates probably will be, too. When you arrive at school, remember that your parents are only a phone call away. If you are homesick, hang in there, pray about it, talk to your friends, and think positive thoughts. Resist the urge to go home. Set a goal to get through the day or the week and don't spend much time alone.

9. "NICE TO MEET YOU!"

Generally speaking, everyone living away at school is friendly and probably as worried as you are in the beginning. If you make an effort to get to know people, they will respond positively. Be friendly. Make this a fresh start.

10. "ON MY HONOR, I WILL TRY, TO DO MY BEST. . ."

If you want a good roommate then be a good roommate and strive to be courteous and thoughtful. Helpful hints: Clean up after yourself. Do not eat others' food. No borrowing of personal items or clothing. Pull your weight (and more). Respect common space. Be aware. Try to be cheerful.

11. THE GOLDEN RULES

1. If you open it, close it.
2. If you turn it on, turn it off.
3. If you unlock it, lock it up.
4. If you break it, admit it.
5. If you can't fix it, call in someone who can.
6. If you borrow it, return it.
7. If you value it, take care of it.
8. If you move it, put it back.
9. If you make a mess, clean it up.
10. If it belongs to someone else, ask to use it.
11. If you don't know how to operate it, leave it alone.
12. If it's none of your business, don't ask questions.

author unknown

NUTRITION, HEALTH & EXERCISE

Lord God,

I am so grateful for Your gift of good health. I know that You protect me every day of my life. I will try to take good care of my body and nourish my soul with Your words. Help me to balance my life. Help me to remember that when I am sick Your healing capabilities are infinite and true. I praise You for giving me strength and protection. In Christ's name,

Amen.

. . . .

Worship the LORD your God,
and his blessing will be on your food and water.
I will take away sickness from among you.
Exodus 23:25

12. WHO'S THE BOSS? . . .YOU ARE!

Nobody will be telling you to eat your green beans. Remember, you are in charge of keeping your body healthy now. What you eat today has a major impact on how your body looks, feels, and functions now and in the future. Be aware and try to make healthy choices.

13. FIFTEEN BELOW

Beware of the "freshman fifteen." Don't be surprised if you put on a few pounds your first year away—most people do. Weight can creep up easily with all-you-can-eat food lines and changes in lifestyle. But don't get too obsessive about your body. Keep a healthy, well-balanced outlook—and exercise!

14. THE FAB FIVE

Eating at least five servings of fruits and vegetables each day is highly recommended by medical and nutrition experts. Think of it as a small personal challenge to try to get the big five in each day.

15. ATTENTION JUNK FOOD JUNKIES!

Fresh fruit, vegetables, and whole grains are real winners for your body. Baked foods are better than fried. And go easy on dressings, sauces, and croissants. Most snack foods are usually high in fat content and sugar, obviously. (Of course, a Twinkie now and then wouldn't be the end of the world!)

16. CHECKS AND BALANCES

Keep yourself in check by maintaining a healthy balance in your life with God, school, friends, family, exercise, and work. If any one of these "pillars" falls, the rest will help support you.

17. FIT AND FIRM

Not only is exercise great for your overall health, it can quicken the mind and stimulate more creative thinking. Keeping fit also helps to reduce stress and seems to help you to sleep better and eat more nutritiously.

18. SLEEPLESS IN SEATTLE. . .BOSTON. . .L.A. . .

Lack of sleep may break down your immune system so your body can be more vulnerable to illness. Try to catch up on missed sleep whenever possible. Take a day off if you need to.

19. DEADLY SERIOUS ABOUT STDs

It may take only *one* sexual intercourse experience with *one* person to become infected with the HIV virus or another sexually transmitted disease (STD). And it may take only *one* sexual intercourse experience to become (or to get someone else) pregnant. One split second, in-the-heat-of-the-moment decision can drastically change your life.

SAFETY

Heavenly Father,

I believe in Your promises to us. You tell us to fear not, that You are always with us. Help me to make intelligent and practical decisions about my life while at the same time releasing any fears I might have to You with the understanding that You are watching over me. You are my light and my salvation. Thank You for Your amazing comfort!

Amen.

. . . .

The LORD is my light and my salvation—
whom shall I fear?
Psalm 27:1

20. HEADS UP

Unfortunately, we live in an imperfect world where unjustified and personal violations can happen. Without being paranoid, use general caution and always be alert to your environment. Employ common sense about things like walking in well-lit areas and being aware of unusual or suspicious behaviors. There will be a campus police department or security force at your college for your safety and protection. Use their help if a need or question arises.

21. LIFE AND DEATH

You will probably find a certain amount of alcohol consumption around your campus. You may or may not feel pressure to follow suit. Obviously, you shouldn't drink and drive or ride with anyone who is "under the influence." If you give in to just one bad decision, it could mess up your entire life. Worse, that same decision could also destroy someone else's life. Be responsible and think long term.

22. KEY MASTER

It takes eight seconds for a thief to enter your room and leave with valuables. Close and lock your dorm room door every time you leave, even for a moment. Over ninety percent of campus room and office thefts involve occupants who were "gone just for a few minutes." And don't lend your keys to anyone.

23. EMERGENCY ONLY

Take this hot tip from Grandma: Always keep a twenty-dollar bill tucked away in your backpack, purse, or wallet for that real emergency—a taxi ride home or whatever. Remember to replace it if you use it.

24. A TURNOFF

Most household appliances do not have automatic shutoffs, so make sure hot pots, coffee makers, and irons are turned off or unplugged when they are not in use. Build a habit of checking every time you leave the room.

25. FIRE ESCAPE

What is your fire or earthquake plan? Know or develop an escape plan from your dorm room or apartment. Discuss the plan with roommates and know escape routes. You might consider having a long rope or rope ladder available for an emergency exit from a multistory building. Be prepared.

26. MOUTH-TO-MOUTH

Take a class in Cardiopulmonary Resuscitation (CPR) or a refresher course if you've already taken one. You could make the difference in the life of a roommate, friend, or family member.

SOCIAL LIFE & DATING

Father,

Thanks for all the relationships You've brought into my life. Help me to be wise and careful in my dating relationships so I can be a good representative of You. Don't let me lose focus on You (something that is easy to do while dating). Bless me with friends who know You, friends who will sharpen my faith in You and be there in hard times. Bless me, also, with friends who do not know You, so that I can shine brightly for You and share with them the joy I've found in You. Mostly, I pray that You'll help me love people better. For that, You said, is how people would know I am Your disciple.

Amen.

. . . .

In everything,
do to others what you would have them do to you,
for this sums up the Law and the Prophets.
Matthew 7:12

27. GO FOR IT!

Involving yourself in study groups, joining clubs, playing sports, attending church or college groups, going to movies, participating in campus and dorm activities and athletic events can make your college years great fun. College is not only academic—your learning will be multidimensional. Get out and meet people. Do everything you have time for while keeping up with your studies.

28. NETWORKING

Learn the names of at least two or three students in each of your classes. Jot their names discreetly in your notebook for that class. You will then easily be reminded of their names at a glance just before the next class to say "hi" or to ask a question.

29. "WHEREFORE ART THOU?"

As you are developing intellectually and socially, you will also want to broaden your horizons culturally. Take a friend and visit museums, art galleries, and historical monuments. Attend local theater productions, operas, and symphonies (on and off campus).

30. BE A SPORT!

Support your school by attending on-campus athletic events. It is a good, inexpensive, and fun way to be entertained. It's also an excellent way to meet other students.

31. FOOD FOR THOUGHT

Before dating someone, talk on the phone for a while before you make plans. On the first date, meet for lunch in a restaurant or public area. It will be safe, less expensive than dinner out, and there will be a more specific time limit on the date.

32. IN HIGH ESTEEM

Studies have shown that individuals with low self-esteem tend to engage in sexual relations beginning at a younger age. Conversely, individuals with high self-esteem tend to have sexual relations beginning when they are older and more mature. Is this a security/insecurity issue? Where do you stand?

33. IT'S TRUE. . .

When dating, remember that the only safe sex is *no* sex.

34. HAPPINESS=MARATHON. . .NOT SPRINT!

Pace yourself. As this is your first time living away from home, enjoy the experience. Don't go crazy and try to pack all your fun into four or five years. You have the rest of your life to have fun, too.

School & Classes

Dear Lord,

Thank You for this great and rare chance to pursue higher education. I hope that in the midst of all the activity, logistics, and details of the world of academia, You'll give me patience and appreciation of where You've placed me. In Jesus' precious name,

Amen.

. . . .

**Whoever loves discipline loves knowledge,
but he who hates correction is stupid.
Proverbs 12:1**

35. ON-THE-JOB-TRAINING

Getting an education is your job right now. Half of that job is to focus on your academics, and the other half is to develop a sense of identity, both personally and socially. When you are feeling burnt-out from studying, remember family members or friends who work a forty- or fifty-hour week and ask yourself, "Have I put in forty hours of studying this week?" This can be a great reality check.

36. IT NEVER HURTS

Fellow classmates can be great resources for you. Ask other students, especially upperclassmen, about the best classes and professors to choose.

37. SYLLABUS SANITY

The syllabus, or course outline, is usually handed out at the first class meeting and will keep you informed of what to expect and remind you of the general guidelines in each of your classes. Keep it in your notebook throughout the term.

38. "THANKS, BUT NO THANKS."

Sharing a textbook with a friend will only cause frustration between partners. It is probably not a great idea.

39. BEST SEAT IN THE HOUSE!

For less distraction and better concentration during a lecture or discussion, sit in the front of the classroom. Get to know your professors by asking a question before or after class or during the instructor's office hours. Developing relationships with professors can enrich your academic experience.

40. CLASS ACT

If you want to enhance your learning, get involved in class discussions, ask questions, and take clear, concise notes. If the instructor looks down at his notes right before speaking, the next sentence will probably be important, so write it down. Read and clean up your notes right after class and think about what you've learned.

41. JUST GO!

Without parents and teachers hovering over you, it's up to you to go to your classes—especially the first few meetings when you're likely to get an overview of what to expect or any changes in the class syllabus. Going to class is the easy part, and it will cut down on your study time. Also, the instructors take it personally when you're not there. So, go!

Study Tips

God,

I know that You are the Author of all things—even of our abilities to think and reason. I pray that I will be a good steward of the gifts You've given me. Help me to do my best without losing sight of You when the pressures of university life rise.

Amen.

. . . .

But as for you, be strong and do not give up,
for your work will be rewarded.
2 Chronicles 15:7

42. "YOU'VE GOTTA BE KIDDING!"

As a full-time college student, studying long hours will become a way of life. As a general rule of thumb, be prepared to study about two to four hours for every hour of class time.

43. A TOTAL TURNOFF

Learning to manage your time well now will help you to be more productive and accomplished in the future. If you want great grades, use your willpower to limit television time and minimize social commitments.

44. STUDY BUDDIES

If you are not self-motivated, study with someone who is smart and serious—someone who will "bug" you to get it done. Get a "personal study trainer."

45. WHAT A TREAT!

Give yourself little rewards during study time for finishing a chapter of reading or upon completion of a rough draft. Make a cup of hot chocolate or take a short walk.

46. READ, LISTEN, AND LEARN

Using your class syllabus or reading list, try to read the assignments before the lecture. The lecture and discussions will be much more meaningful.

47. A BIT COMPULSIVE?

Develop a habit of reviewing what you learned after each class. Write out a paragraph or page of what you recall from the lecture after class. Then check your original notes or textbook and change your recall notes as needed. Reread this review and your notes just before the next class. This habit should increase your learning and retention.

48. JUST DO IT!

If you have a paper due at the end of the semester or quarter, try to complete it as early as possible so as not to increase your anxiety level during final exam time. If you start early, you will also have a better shot at gathering your books and materials before the other students get to them.

49. TESTING TIPS

It is your responsibility to make sure you are fed, watered, pumped up, and ready to go before an exam. Be fully aware of exam dates and be prepared. Have test materials like blue-books and calculators with you.

Keeping the Faith

Dear Father,

Please hold my hand through these exciting years. Help me make choices that will glorify You. I pray that I am the consummate ambassador of Your love and that You will be proud of the way I live my life. Thank You for the eternal love and life You promise us through the life of Your Son, Jesus.

Amen.

. . . .

Be self-controlled and alert.
Your enemy the devil prowls around
like a roaring lion looking for
someone to devour.
Resist him, standing firm in the faith.
1 Peter 5:8–9

50. LET'S GO SHOPPING!

Find a new church as soon as possible, even if you are planning to become involved in a campus-based Christian group. Ask people about churches in the area. Consider geographic location, denominational preference, and transportation issues. Is it a good fit for you in terms of its style of worship? Does it offer an active college group?

51. PARTY ANYONE?

Campus Crusade and Intervarsity are nationwide Christian organizations for college students. One or both should be represented on your campus. Take a friend and try out all of the welcome events the first month of school. You should see flyers and posters around campus and in residence halls. There may be small gatherings, barbecues, and parties for you to learn what these groups offer and to give you an opportunity to meet other students. These groups can make a large university seem a lot smaller.

52. THE WORD

The Scriptures can help you to make wise decisions as you begin your venture into the "real world." Studying your Bible will certainly help to keep you on track during these next few powerful years. A Bible study group will be valuable to help you learn what God wants you to know. It's a great way to meet new friends and empower you in your knowledge of the Word.

53. CAUTION. . .FALLING OBJECTS

None of us are free from temptation. Some of the biggest temptations of your life will come during your college experiences. Be assertive about getting plugged into a family of believers who will support you and with whom you can talk about the challenges of living away from home.

54. SOUL MUSIC

Listen to Christian music if you have a choice. There are radio stations that play incredible spiritual music, or you can enjoy some of the great compact discs by Christian artists. It's all just another way to praise God.

55. KEEPING TIDY

As difficult as it is in today's world, try to be cautious about what enters your mind and spirit. Be wary of movies, songs, television shows, and gossip. Stay on high ground.

56. HIGH GROUND

Live your life and act as if Jesus is standing right beside you at all times, watching every movement and listening to every word you utter. He is!

Money Matters

Dear Lord,

Realizing that the management of money is an earthly challenge, help me always to keep my priorities in good order with You at the top of the list. Guide me in my management of what You have so generously given to me. Remind me that there are people much less fortunate who need my help, too. You tell us that the love of money is not good and that true joy is found in the great depth of Your profound love. Help us to enjoy Your grace and the eternal life You've given.

Amen.

. . . .

**A faithful man will be richly blessed,
but one eager to get rich will not go unpunished.
Proverbs 28:20**

57. MAKE CENTS?

Decisions regarding money and banking need to be made before you leave for school. It makes life easier if you open a bank account in your college town that has a branch in your hometown as well. Or, open an account in your hometown before you leave, making sure there is a branch in your college town.

58. PAPER AND PLASTIC

Inquire at your new bank about opening a student account. You will probably want only a checking account (with duplicate checks) and an ATM card for cash withdrawals.

59. "I'VE GOT A SECRET!"

Keep your secret ATM code a secret! Try to use your ATM card only during daylight hours, for safety reasons. It will also be helpful to devise a recording system to keep track of all ATM cash withdrawals. It is easy to forget to record withdrawals—and that can make a mess of your bank accounts.

60. DO LEAVE HOME WITHOUT THEM!

Make a pact with yourself not to spend money that you don't have. It is probably best to avoid credit cards at this time in your life. Don't get sucked into the free merchandise and other promotions meant to entice you into the credit world.

61. GET REAL!

Anyone can let spending get out of control. Work out a personal budget to monitor your expenses. Typical budget areas include housing, food, utilities, transportation, entertainment, and miscellaneous (haircuts, laundry, clothing, school supplies, gifts, etc.). Be realistic and put it on paper.

62. LOAN SHARKS

It's tempting to take out student loans (many people do) and keep the spending up—but you're not dealing with a loan from Aunt Jill. Remember, everything you borrow and spend must be paid back eventually. A bank or loan company will definitely want the money (plus interest) back. Be conservative and try to stay as debt-free as possible.

Organization

Jesus,

Teach me to manage what You have given me. Make my hands productive in the work and the life You have chosen for me now. Let my excitement about Your promises fill me with energy and enthusiasm and let Your Spirit spread to others through me.

Amen.

. . . .

Lazy hands make a man poor,
but diligent hands bring wealth.
Proverbs 10:4

63. PLOT YOUR COURSE

Getting organized in the beginning can save you a lot of time and worry in the long run. During the first week of the term, plot your classes on a large calendar or on your computer. Fill in due dates, project and paper deadlines, exam dates, reading assignments, and study group times. Stay on track!

64. AT A GLANCE

Your life will most likely get busier and more complicated as you get older. Build a habit of carrying a small pocket calendar with you. Fill in important days (birthdays, anniversaries, etc.), dates, appointments, and meetings. Include study times as well as social commitments. In the back, keep phone numbers, frequent flyer account numbers, and anything else for quick reference (except your ATM code!). Prepare for your day by glancing at the calendar and to-do list as you get started each morning. Writing everything down will help you follow through with commitments and relieve you of the stress of trying to remember on your own.

65. "CLEAR" UP YOUR ACT

A "stitch in time" will allow you to think more clearly and get more accomplished. Keep your desk or study area as clean as possible to cut distractions. Designate a place for everything. Label boxes, shelves, baskets, file drawers, and cabinets. Your trash can will help, too.

66. QUARTERS REQUIRED

You will find that you will need quarters (and dollar bills) for many things—soft drink and snack machines, newspapers, phone calls, and laundry. Save your quarters. Have a quarter can or jar in your room and guard it with your life!

67. WARM OR COLD?

A good rule of thumb for doing laundry is to use warm water. Most detergents will function fine in cold water, too, but stay away from hot water at this point in your career.

68. IRON HAND

After washing and drying your clothes and linens, remove them from dryer immediately making sure they are totally dry and still warm. Then, as you fold them (while warm) you can use your hand as an "iron" to smooth out the wrinkles and make creases where they belong.

69. WRINKLE FREE

There is a tendency to pack the dryer full of clothes to save money and time. Limit the amount of clothing in the dryer. Hot tip: fewer clothes, fewer wrinkles.

General Success

Lord,

You are my light and my salvation. You are the true example of excellence. Guide me where I go and remind me that I am always a representative of You. I know that my character, integrity, and self-respect do show through in my behavior. To me, the ultimate sign of success is to live a life that pleases You.

Amen.

. . . .

But seek first his kingdom and his righteousness,
and all these things will be given to you as well.
Matthew 6:33

70. STRIVE FOR EXCELLENCE

Successful people set goals for themselves. The most successful people write their goals. If you decide to set goals for yourself, develop them around your own personal standards and not by the standards of your friends and classmates. You can write short-term, five-year, and lifetime goals. Always strive to do and be your personal best.

71. "THANK YOU, GOD!"

Be truly thankful for the gifts in your life. Grateful people are happy people. Remember to consistently express your gratitude to God, your family, and your friends for all the good things in your life—love and support, good health, educational opportunities, etc.

72. A FINAL THOUGHT

With all the tough decisions, temptations, and problems you will encounter during your college days and throughout your life, remember to live your life in such a way that, someday, you will be proud to tell your children everything—should they ask. (And they will!)

PACKING CHECKLIST

CLOTHING

___ T-shirts
___ Jeans
___ Sweats
___ Collar shirts or blouses
___ Sweaters
___ Blazer
___ Slacks/long pants
___ Skirts & dresses (a few)
___ Turtlenecks
___ Shorts
___ Underwear (a lot)
___ Tights & pantyhose
___ Thermal undies

___ Socks
___ Baseball hats
___ Pajamas
___ Heavy jacket
___ Hooded jacket
___ Belt(s)
___ Sneakers
___ Comfy shoes
___ Dressy shoes
___ Flip-flops
___ Slippers
___ Bathrobe
___ Athletic wear

PERSONAL ITEMS

___ Shampoo
___ Conditioner
___ Soap
___ Shaving cream
___ Razor
___ Toothbrush
___ Toothpaste

___ Curling iron
___ Q-tips
___ Nail polish
___ Polish remover
___ Toenail clippers
___ Emery boards
___ Bible

___ Deodorant

___ Dental floss

___ Sunscreen

___ Lotion

___ Make-up

___ Hairspray

___ Shower container

___ Hydrogen peroxide

___ Hair dryer

___ Kleenex

___ Cold/flu medicine

___ Hairbrush/comb

___ Tampons/pads

___ Tylenol or Advil

___ Neosporin

___ Bandages

___ Cologne

___ Vitamins

___ Lip balm

___ Umbrella

HOUSEHOLD THINGS

___ Sheet set(s)

___ Blankets

___ Bed pillow

___ Mattress pad

___ Washcloths (3–5)

___ Radio

___ Desk lamp

___ Throw rug

___ Utensils

___ Popcorn popper (opt.)

___ Dish soap

___ Posters, pillows, plants

___ Fabric softening strips

___ Quarters for laundry

___ Quilt/bedspread

___ Towels (3–5)

___ Small sewing kit

___ Flashlight

___ Iron

___ Alarm clock

___ Power strip

___ Plastic dishes

___ Coffee mugs

___ Flower vase

___ Laundry soap

___ Laundry basket

___ Stain remover

___ Windex

___ Paper towels
___ Storage crates or boxes
___ Telephone
___ Answering machine
___ Mini tool kit
___ Hooks & tacks
___ Bulletin board

___ Security lock
___ Tapes & CD's
___ Garbage bags
___ Broom
___ Hammer & nails
___ Dry erase board
___ Waste basket

SCHOOL SUPPLIES

___ White bond paper
___ Notebooks or binders
___ Pens (12)
___ Thesaurus
___ Staples
___ Tape dispenser
___ Transparent ruler
___ Large paper clips
___ Colored marking pens
___ Post-it note pads
___ Electric pencil sharpener
___ Address book
___ File folders
___ Calculator
___ Large calendar

___ Notebook paper
___ Pencils (12)
___ Dictionary
___ Stapler
___ Scotch tape
___ Scissors
___ Glue sticks
___ Liquid Paper
___ Small notepads
___ Stationery
___ Envelopes
___ Roll of stamps
___ File boxes or crates
___ Pocket calendar
___ Good backpack